FIX

YOUR

CLOTHES

the sustainable magic of mending, patching, and darning

raleigh briggs

Microcosm Publishing
Portland, OR

FIX YOUR CLOTHES

written and illustrated by

raleigh briggs

ISBN 978-1-62106-906-5
This is Microcosm #123

Distributed by Perseus Books Group + Turnaround, UK

Microcosm Publishing
2752 N Williams Ave
Portland, OR 97227

microcosmpublishing.com

Names: Briggs, Raleigh, author, illustrator.
Title: Fix your clothes : the sustainable magic of mending, patching, and
    darning / Raleigh Briggs.
Description: Portland, OR : Microcosm Publishing, 2017.
Identifiers: LCCN 2016035225 (print) | LCCN 2016036282 (ebook) | ISBN
    9781621069065 (paperback) | ISBN 9781621061618 (e-pdf) | ISBN
    9781621069195 (epub) | ISBN 9781621068471 (mobi/kindle)
Subjects: LCSH: Clothing and dress--Repairing--Handbooks, manuals, etc. |
    BISAC: CRAFTS & HOBBIES / Sewing. | CRAFTS & HOBBIES / Fashion. |
    REFERENCE / Handbooks & Manuals. | CRAFTS & HOBBIES / Reference.
Classification: LCC TT720 .B75 2017 (print) | LCC TT720 (ebook) | DDC
    646.4--dc23
LC record available at https://lccn.loc.gov/2016035225

In this little zine, we'll be talking about clothes. Unless you wear seamless, zipperless, indestructible coveralls (email me if you do!), you've had to deal with the fact that clothes are mortal. We love them, but they fail us in myriad ways. Whether you buy new or used clothing, you have to deal with the seam that busts when you bend over. The zipper that slips down to reveal your underpants to your coworkers. The cute and cheap outfit that turns out to be just ... cheap.

All of these things are annoying, but none of them have to ruin your day. Even if you haven't sewn so much as a pillowcase, it's worth your time to learn a few basic clothing repairs. You don't have to buy new jeans every time the inner thighs wear out — just patch them up and keep rocking them! You'll save money, save those jeans from premature death in some landfill, and create something that is, in its own humble way, uniquely yours. Your first few projects might look goofy, it's true, but they'll still look better than giant holes in your clothes. So let's get started.

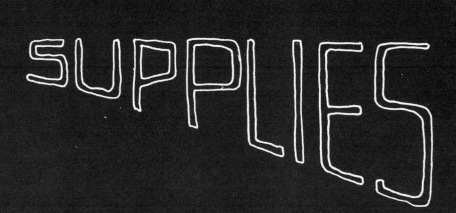

Just a few little things you'll need before you start sewing:

Needles

A good multipack of needles can get you through most DIY fixes. You'll need some thin needles (for delicate fabrics) and a few thicker ones for mending denim or canvas.

Thimble

If you think you don't need a thimble, just try to hem some jeans without crying.

Thread

If you're just beginning to sew, the thread section of the fabric store can induce a feeling of "thread panic," a term I just made up. Thread comes in all different thicknesses, colors, and fibers, and it can be hard to know what to pick for your project.

If you're just doing basic mending and alteration, you should be fine with just a couple of spools. Cotton-wrapped polyester thread will give you the most versatility for your buck. It's strong, heat-resistant, and will work on most fabrics. Get a spool each of white, black, and whatever color is most dominant in your wardrobe.

Seam Ripper

The sharp mandibles of a seam ripper undo stitches gracefully,

without tugging. Use the blunt-tip side to loosen a stitch, then flip the ripper over and use the sharp prong to cut the thread.

Measuring Tape + Ruler

The fancy clear rulers are especially nice for sewing. Any tape measure will do as long as it's flexible.

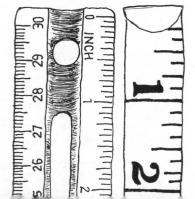

Tailor's Chalk

You can pick up a couple hunks of fabric chalk at your favorite craft store. Some of them even come with little brushes that erase the marks when you're done. If chalk's not your thing, you can also find markers that wash out.

Notions

These will depend on what sorts of clothes you like to wear, but a well-stocked notions stash usually contains two- and four-hole buttons, hook & eye sets, zippers, snaps, and patches.

Beeswax

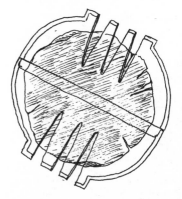

Folks who hand-sew use beeswax to add strength and glide to their thread. To do this, hold one end of your thread against the wax, with your finger a couple inches from the thread's tip. Grab the short end of the thread with your other hand and pull the whole length of the thread across the wax. (Most commercial waxes have holders with little guides to keep the thread from slipping off.) Do this a couple times so that the thread is nicely coated.

Next, run over your thread with a warm iron to melt the wax into the thread. This might seem fussy, but the ironing is important — it removes any waxy residue and creates a strong, tangle-free thread with plenty of glide.

Pins & A Pincushion

Buy a tin of straight pins with the little pearls on the ends. Keeping a couple dozen in a pin-cushion will keep you from having to pull a single pin from a pile of bloodthirsty ones.

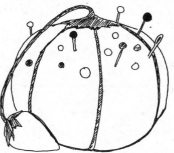

Fabric Scissors

A modest but decent-quality pair is all you need. You needn't spend tons of money, but if you want your scissors to stay sharp, avoid using them to cut anything other than fabric. Paper, plastic, or cardboard can make the blades too blunt.

Quick Fixes!

Sometimes you absolutely don't have time to sew on a button, and that's okay. Walking around with buttonless pants, however, is probably not okay. You can avoid these little mishaps by creating an emergency mending kit, filled with McGyver-y supplies to hold you over until you can do some real mending. Reach for it next time your (totally rhetorical) jeans button pops off post-breakfast burrito and it's making you late for work.

A few things to add to your kit:

* safety pins for popped buttons + "librarian's gaps"

* Fray Check (a liquid plastic that stops fabric from fraying)

* Iron-on hemming tape or double-sided tape

* a few cute pins or pin-on buttons (for strategic stain coverage)

* a mini-stapler, for VERY quick n'dirty hem fixes

Basic Knots + Stitches

Knots! And stitches! You need to learn a few of them. But don't be nervous. Hand-sewing does require a bit of motor skill, but mostly it requires you to be patient, or at least to have a good movie to watch while you're working. The fineness and evenness of your stitches will improve with practice, so jump right in!

If you already sew a bit, feel free to skip ahead. If you're a newbie, here are some basic stitches you should learn.

Starter's Knot

Every sewing project starts with a single knot. Beginning sewers tend to make their knots really big, hoping this will keep the knot from pulling through the fabric. But a big knot can get tangled in your other stitches. It also uses a bunch of thread that can be put to better use elsewhere. Also it looks weird! So save yourself the trouble and keep your knot simple. Make a slipknot at the end of your thread. Take the needle through the loop and pull the rest of the thread through. Then, pinch the whole shebang between your thumb and forefinger and slide the knot to the end of the thread until it's tight.

Tying Off

Again, don't waste your time tying tons of knots to secure your work. To make a knot that lays flat and doesn't bunch, first bring your thread and needle to the wrong side of the fabric. Make a tiny stitch that's perpendicular to your other stitches, pull the thread most of the way through, then take your needle under the thread that's left. Pull the thread tight-ish and repeat with another stitch. Make sure your thread is secure, then snip the thread to ½ inch.

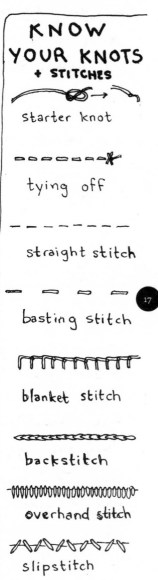

KNOW YOUR KNOTS + STITCHES

starter knot

tying off

straight stitch

basting stitch

blanket stitch

backstitch

overhand stitch

slipstitch

17

Straight Stitch

Use it to: join two pieces of fabric; make simple hems; gather fabric

As basic as it gets! Thread your needle, make a knot at one end, and push the needle from the wrong side to the right side of the fabric. Then, use your needle to weave through the fabric in a straight line, creating a few stitches. Try to keep your stitches even. Pull your thread through (try not to bunch the fabric) and repeat as needed.

Basting Stitch

Use it to: hold your fabric in place while you're sewing — like straight pins, but less pokey

A basting stitch is pretty much a long, loose straight stitch. When you baste, use a thread in a contrasting color so that you can easily find and remove the stitches later.

Blanket Stitch

Use it to: make a decorative edging; attach two pieces of fabric along their edges

Thread your needle and take it from wrong to right side through the edge of the garment so that the needle comes out the bottom.

Take the needle over the edge of the fabric (so it's behind the fabric again) and bring it through again at a point a little ways over and above from where you brought the thread through the first time. Move your needle so that it's inside the loop formed by the stitch you just made, and pull the thread through. If you're right-handed, you'll see that the stitch forms a backwards L. Lefties will see a regular L. Make another stitch by taking your needle over the edge to the back of the fabric, coming through to the front, catching the needle, and pulling through.

Backstitch

Use it to: mend seams; replace zippers

Backstitching gives you a tight, strong line without any gaps, so it's great for decorative stitching, too. A caveat: backstitching looks crappy from the wrong side of the fabric, so don't use it on anything that needs to be reversible.

To create a backstitch, start like you're making a straight stitch. Bring your needle up as if you're making a second stitch, but instead of bringing your needle forward along the seam you're making, bring the needle back about a half stitch's length and insert your needle through the middle of the stitch to the back of the fabric. Angle your needle forward and bring the tip to the front about a half stitch's length in front of where you first brought the thread through. Pull the needle and thread through all the way.

Make the next stitch by bringing the point of your needle backwards again and inserting it from front to back at the halfway mark of your first stitch. Again, angle your needle forward and bring the point to the front a half stitch ahead of your last stitch. Pull everything through and continue like this until you're done.

Overhand Stitch/Whipstitch

Use it to: finish an edge; create a buttonhole

An overhand stitch is done over the edge of your fabric, rather than parallel to an edge. Bring your needle up through the fabric about ¼ inch from the edge, then wrap it around the fabric's edge and back to the wrong side. Bring your needle up again in a spot that's very close to your previous stitch and pull the thread through. This way you'll create a tight row of stitches that "seal" the edge of the fabric in thread.

Slipstitch

Use it to: create an invisible hem

A very classy stitch that's great for making hems in delicate or fancy clothes. To make a slip-stitch, start by holding your basted hem horizontally. Slip your thread under one or two threads from the outer fabric (the part that's not folded), and then, moving forward a little along the hem, pick up two threads from the folded portion of the hem. Head back up to the outer fabric, create a teeny stitch like before, then repeat with the inner fabric. Continue making this delicate little zigzag until your hem is complete.

TIP!: Are you having trouble making a straight line? You can use a ruler and tailor's chalk to create a guide before you start sewing.

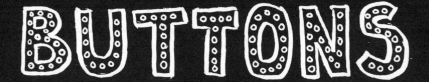

Even if you don't plan on ever making your own clothes, it's imperative that you learn how to sew on a button. Because inevitably there will come a time when a missing button is what keeps you from wearing your favorite interview skirt, cardigan, catsuit, or whatever. Sure, a safety pin will do in a pinch, but come on.

Let's sew buttons!

Flat Buttons

If your button's destiny is to close a shirt, secure a pocket, or just look pretty, a flat button will do the trick.

Step 1: Grab your garment, a button, a needle, and six inches of thread. If you're picky, make sure to choose thread that matches the thread used on the other buttons. Pick a thin needle that can easily fit into the holes of the button.

Step 2: Cut 6-10 inches of thread. Wax your thread if you like. Thread the needle and pull half the thread through. Then, use an overhand knot to tie the ends of the thread together.

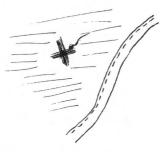

Step 3: Pick where you'd like to place your button.

Step 4: Insert the needle into the fabric on the wrong side (the side that faces in toward your body). Pop the button on top and pull the needle through.

Step 5: Go back down through the opposite hole you came up through. Repeat! Repeat 4 or 5 times more.

Step 6: If your button has four holes, repeat steps 4 and 5 on the other two holes. End with your needle on the wrong side of the fabric and the thread pulled all the way through.

Step 7: Tie an overhand knot in the thread, as close to the fabric as you can get. Snip the thread. You're all done!

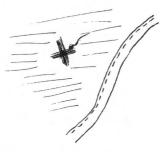

25

Shank Buttons

If your garment is made of thicker material (like denim or canvas), you should use a shank button. Instead of holes in its face, a shank button has a raised area or loop on the back. Shank buttons are also used for the flies of pants and other *high-stress* areas (heh).

When you're placing or replacing a shank button, upgrade from all-purpose to quilting thread—it's a lot stronger and comes in a billion colors, just like all-purpose.

Step 1: Start with about 2 feet of thread, a thickish needle, beeswax (if using), a thimble, and a small, clear button (optional).

Step 2: Wax your thread (extra important if you're using all-purpose thread instead of something stronger). Thread your needle, pull half of the thread through and knot both ends of the thread together, creating a strong double thread.

Step 3: Choose where you will place your button and bring the needle up from the wrong side of the fabric. Make a few small stitches over your chosen spot before you add the button.

/// = wrong side!

Step 4: Place the small, clear button on the inside of the garment, on top of the stitches you just made. Anchor this button with a few stitches. This will help add stability to your shank button and cut down on fabric wear later on.

Step 5: Hold your shank button in place on the outside of the garment and tack it in place with a few semi-tight

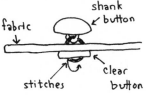

fabric

shank button

stitches

clear button

stitches. Make sure you're sewing these same stitches in the clear button on the other side.

NOTE: Don't pull your thread tight when you make these stitches. If you can't help it, slide a toothpick under the button's shank while you stitch.

Step 6: After you have 5 or 6 stitches holding your buttons in place, pull the needle one more time to the fabric's right side, then wrap the thread around the stitches holding the shank in place. Do this several times.

Step 7: Make a teeny loop in the thread on the needle; hold it with a finger. Bring the needle around the shank and through the loop, then pull the thread tight. Repeat this a few times.

Step 8: Finally, bring your needle back to the wrong side, knot off + snip your thread.

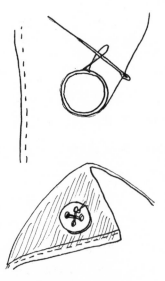

TIPS! A lot of garments come with a spare button, either in a baggie or stitched into the garment in an inconspicuous place. Before you buy new buttons, check the tails and insides for a spare.

Also, when you spill ink on a shirt or its armpits rot out, cut off all the buttons before you scrap it. Now you have a free set of buttons. You're welcome!

Mending Seams

If you could choose a way for your clothes to break, you'd pick a busted seam. Fixing a seam is a piece of cake! The pieces of fabric are already lined up and held in place by the stitches that didn't bust, and most of the time you don't have to deal with damaged fabric. Seams are easy to fix even if your not the world's greatest stitcher, so don't be intimidated by the prospect of having to sew in a straight line.

Prep

First things first! Check out your seam. Did the seam tear because the thread holding it together broke, or because the fabric around the seam was too damaged to hold? If you're dealing with torn or damaged fabric, skip ahead to the section on patching. You'll need to patch over the missing bits first and then incorporate that fabric into your seam.

No damage? Sweet. Use a double knot to tie off the threads on either side of your open seam. The knot should be snug, but not so tight that it causes the rest of the seam to bunch up.

Trim the ends of the knots so that they don't poke through to the other side. This is important: A seam with uneven stitches can still pass as charming; a seam with squiggly threads poking out just looks dumb.

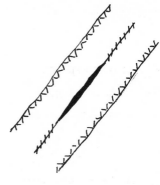

Press

If you have time, press your seam open before you start mending. This will help you keep track of your seam allowances (the distance between the seam and the fabric's edge) and give you a neat, perfect seam.

If you don't care about looking perfect, I don't blame you. Read on.

Pin

Even if you're in a hurry, *please* don't forget to pin your seam before you start sewing. I can't stress this enough! Pins will keep the fabric together so you can concentrate on sewing a straight line and keeping your stitches even.

To pin, turn your garment inside out (if you hadn't already), find the busted part of the seam, and line up the edges of the fabric. Bridge the gap in the seam by placing pins perpendicular to the edge of the fabric, tips pointing out.

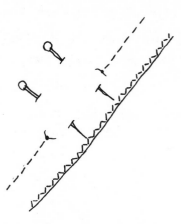

What? You're in a hurry AND all your pins fell into the toilet? Use clear or masking tape, folded over both edges of the fabric.

Stitch

Begin your stitching about 3/4 inch before the missing part of the seam, to ensure there won't be a gap between the old seam and your new one.

Then, just stitch a new seam where the old seam was. Use the holes of the old seam as a guide. Remove your pins as you work.

Use a backstitch or small straight stitches — whatever fits closest with the rest of the seam. Sew about 3/4 inch beyond the gap on the other end, then knot and snip your thread.

Finish

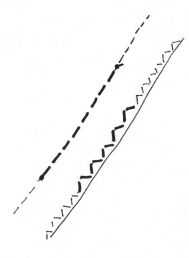

Check the edge of your fabric. Is it finished with a zigzag or overhand stitch? If so, did these stitches come undone when your seam ripped? Keeping those edges unfinished can leave your fabric vulnerable to fraying.

If you have the time, replacing those finishing stitches with a quick zigzag or overhand stitch of your own will keep the fabric from unraveling. There's no sense in mending a seam just to fix it again when the fabric unravels!

P.S., you can also treat a fabric's edges with a drop or two of Fray Check, which you can find at the fabric store.

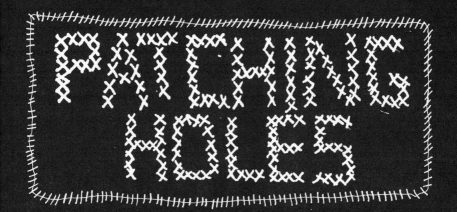

Torn or worn-through fabric is a different mending experience than, say, an unraveled seam. Because a hole can weaken the fabric around it, you can't just sew it up with a row of stitches. Instead, you have two options: patch it or darn it. Sewing on a patch is often preferable to darning the hole itself.

DO NOT be seduced by the lure of the iron-on patch! Iron-ons might seem easy, but the adhesive is always jacked, and your fabric + color choices are depressing. Patching is an art form, and those tan drugstore patches are the equivalent of Thomas Kinkade paintings. Avoid at all costs!

When you choose a patch, find a fabric that's similar to that of what you're mending. Match exactly if you can, but at least find something with a similar weight and stretch. As for color, that's really up to you! If you want an exact match, you can use fabric from the garment itself to patch the hole. Just sew up a seldom-used pocket (such as the back or coin pockets in a pair of jeans) and cut a little fabric away from the layer underneath the pocket.

HOW TO PATCH *The Fancy Way*

Step 1: Trim away the fabric around the hole until it's a nice square. Snip a ¼ inch slit in each corner and fold these flaps inside the garment so it forms a "frame" around the hole on the wrong side of the fabric. Iron these flaps so they stay.

Step 2: Cut enough patch fabric to extend at least ½ inch beyond the hole on all sides. If your patch and garment are printed, align them in a way that looks good to you. Iron the patch and pin it over the hole, matching the grain of the fabrics. Try not to stretch or bunch the fabric. You can also baste the patch in place.

Step 3: Thread your need with a double length of thread and tie the ends together. Fold back the extra ½ inch of patch fabric on one side and, using tiny diagonal stitches, sew the fold of the patch fabric to the folded edge of the garment fabric. Stitch all the way around the hole + knot off.

Step 4: Finish by tacking down the edges of the patch with little zigzag stitches. Only pick up a few threads with each stitch. Knot off and snip any loose threads. Done!

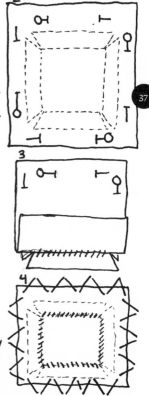

HOW TO PATCH THE QUICK & DIRTY WAY

AKA the punk-patch special. Who needs hidden stitches?

Step 1: Snip any loose or hanging threads from around the hole. Pin on your patch, matching the grain of the fabrics. Try not to bunch or stretch the fabric, if you can help it.

Step 2: Thread your needle with a double length of thread and tie the ends together. Start at one corner of the patch and bring your needle up from underneath. From there, stich around all the edges of the patch using either diagonal stitches or blanket stitches. Try to keep your stitches even and loose enough to not tug on the patch fabric. End with your needle on the wrong side of the fabric and knot off. Done done done!

1

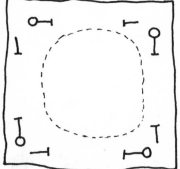

2

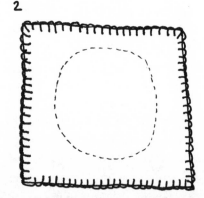

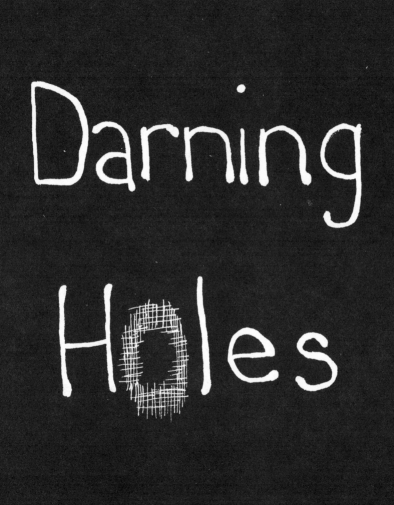

What, you're not satisfied with just slapping a patch on your pants and calling it a day? You want to actually *fix* the hole? WELL FINE.

When you darn a hole, you're using thread to weave a tiny bit of cloth to replace what's been lost. This is a little tedious to accomplish, but if you want to keep wearing that favorite pair of socks, it's totally worth it.

/// = crappily done wood grain effect!

A DARNING EGG

Darning is easiest if you acquire a thing called a darning egg. It looks like a chicken egg with a handle attached. The egg works by providing a surface for the fabric to lie on top of, so that the edges of the hole don't get distorted. If you don't have a darning egg, you can place your non-sewing hand underneath the fabric — just try not to stretch or bunch the fabric as you work.

Step 1: Place the darning egg (or your hand) underneath the hole.

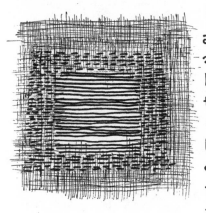

Step 2: Using strong thread and a darning needle, create a running stitch that begins beneath and to one side of the hole and goes straight across. When you're a little beyond the opposite edge of the hole, turn around and start a new stitch in the opposite direction. Work back and forth until you have a little square of horizontal stitches that extends beyond the hole on all sides.

Step 3: Without tying off, shift directions, and begin to weave by creating a vertical line of stitches over and under the horizontal stitches. Work back and forth, moving left to right (or vice versa) until all your horizontall stitches have been covered by vertical stitches. Knot off your thread and snip. Voila!

41

Ah, hemming! The ultimate wardrobe-stretching skill. A good hem turns a bunchy, ratty-cuffed pair of pants into shorts you can wear for another few years. It's an essential skill for thrift shoppers, swappers, hand-me-downers, and anyone else who hates shopping for clothes. Learn to hem and watch the textile world open to you like a giant, machine-washable oyster.

The Equipment

seam ripper
tailor's chalk
straight pins
yardstick

buddy and/or dress dummy
iron and ironing board
scissors
needles

thread — hem thread and a contrasting color for basting

Step 1

Use a seam ripper to gently release the existing hem. Pull out all the little thread squigglies as best you can without damaging the fabric.

Step 2:

Put on the garment along with shoes you plan on wearing with it. Grab a friend and some tailor's chalk to mark where you want your hem to fall. If you're hemming a skirt or dress, use a yardstick to measure the distance between the hem and the floor.— make sure it's even all the way around. Mark the hem using chalk or straight pins placed parallel to the bottom edge of the fabric.

NOTE: No friends around? Consider getting yourself a dress dummy.

Step 3: Now, undress again
and check your hem marks to make sure they're even. Do both pant legs match up? Does the hemline on that skirt wobble a little?

If your marks are uneven, use a clean toothbrush (or your finger) to erase the mark, and redraw it. Pin the new hem in place, put the garment back on, and check the hem again. Readjust as needed.

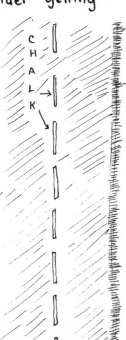

Step 4: Once you're happy
with the hem length,
remove the pins and trim the
bottom of the skirt/pant legs
to their new length plus
an extra 1½-2 inches for your
hem allowance.

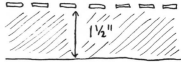

Then, create your new
hem! Fold the bottom edge
of your fabric up ½ inch,
tucking the fabric inside.
Press this lightly, then fold
the fabric again up to the
new hemline. Press again.

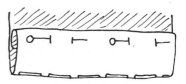

Your chalk line should be on the very bottom
edge of your garment. Pin the hem in place and
baste to tack it down.

Step 5: Choose your
stitch! If you're hemming
casual clothes like jeans or
a sundress, top-stitch your
hem using very small, even
stitches. Make sure to choose
a different color of thread
than your basting thread.
Once you're done, tie off

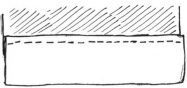

VS.

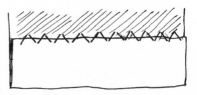

46

your thread on the wrong side of the fabric and remove your basting stitches.

If you're hemming dress pants or a garment on which a topstitched hem would look goofy, you should opt for an invisible hem. Baste first, then use a slipstitch to sew your new hem. See page   for instructions on how to create the discreet and lovely slipstitch.

Tips and Tricks!

★ If your hem looks a little fat, you can blame that first fold you made in your fabric. We do this because the fabric's raw edge can unravel if it's left hanging out. If you finish your edge with a quick overhand stitch, you can skip that first fold and thin out your hem.

★ Hems in knit fabrics like jersey are especially prone to coming undone. Hedge your bets by sewing twin hems, parallel to each other and about 1/4 inch apart.

★ Puckered hems can usually be pressed or steamed out.

Thousands of years of clothing technology and the zipper is still around? Ah, well. Here's how to resolve a few of the most common zipper mishaps.

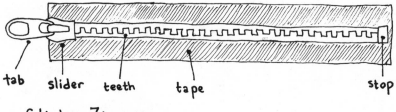

tab   slider   teeth   tape   stop

Sticky Zippers

First, if there is anything actually sticky on

your pants, please wash it off. If your zipper still isn't working smoothly, you'll need to employ a non-messy lubricant to get the slider moving again. Your best bets are a bar of soap or the lead of a graphite pencil. Rub the soap or pencil up and down both sets of teeth, then zip and unzip a few times to get the stuff equally distributed. Wipe off any extra soap or graphite with a clean cloth. You may have to re-lube every few washes.

Slippy Zippers

If your zipper won't stay up, hold it in place with a finger and then shoot the teeth with a quick burst of hairspray. Yep. Try just a tiny bit at first to see if that fixes the problem, then add more if you need it. If you do this to a garment while you're wearing it (I have done this many times) you may want to shield the rest of your outfit with a towel.

Stuck Zippers

This one's pretty easy. There's probably a thread or a bit of fabric caught in your zipper. Grab some tweezers and fish it out. *Don't* try and force the slider past it. Be patient! Tug the slider around gently until you can see the obstruction and remove it.

No Tab (or Broken Tab)

You can fix a broken tab by squeezing the loop closed with some needle-nose pliers, but honestly? My favorite solution is to just replace the tab with a little bit of ribbon, canvas, or leather.

Slider Comes Off Part-way

Step 1: Use a seam ripper and carefully undo the stitches that tack the zipper tape to your garment. Use needle-nose pliers to remove the metal stop from the bottom of the zipper. Slide the slider off of the zipper.

Step 2: Carefully realign the teeth one by one and feed the teeth back into the slider. Go slow to make sure that the teeth are locking together properly. Zip the zipper up all the way.

Step 3: Use a needle and strong thread to make 10 or so tight stitches where the metal stop used to be. This will function as your new stop. Knot your thread well and snip it close so it doesn't get tangled in the zipper.

Gaps Below the Slider

This one is the worst! Sometimes you can hold one set of teeth firmly and nudge the other side up gently until they realign. But when things really go awry, you need to disassemble the bottom of the zipper.

Step 1: Grab your needle-nose pliers and remove the metal stop at the bottom of the zipper.

Step 2: Move the slider carefully down the zipper until it's right below the last pair of teeth. Don't remove the slider from the zipper, though!

Step 3: Smooth out the sides of the zipper and line up the teeth one by one. Feed the teeth slowly through the slider until you can see that they're locking up below.

Step 4: Create a new stop using strong thread, like you did in Step 3 on the previous page (the Slider Comes Off Partway section).

WATER PROOFING

Waterproofing Canvas

Canvas is a beautiful thing, but when it mingles with rain it can quickly become a mildew-speckled, sour-smelling disgrace. Removing mildew is probably not going to happen (ADMIT IT) so it's smart to avoid the nasty stuff altogether. It's pretty easy to make your own waterproofing formulas that you can use on tents, rucksacks, and any other piece of canvas that gets routinely exposed to the elements.

*Before you head off with that jug o' shellac, some caveats:

1. Waterproof canvas will keep rain off your back, but it will keep *in* all your sweat and body heat. So think long and heartily before you waterproof clothing.

2. Natural ≠ friendly. Unlike the recipes from Make Your Place, some of these formulas aren't exactly nontoxic. Do your waterproofing outside, wear gloves and old clothes, and keep kids and animals from getting into what you're making.

3. Don't inhale, eat, mainline, or otherwise absorb your waterproofing formulas.

WATERPROOFING SPRAY *makes enough for one smallish tent

Mix together <u>2 cups soybean oil</u> and <u>1 cup turpentine</u> in a small bucket. Once the two liquids are blended, pour it in a spray bottle (use a funnel) and spray it onto your fabric. Or, keep the stuff in the bucket and paint it onto the canvas with a brush or sponge. Use half the batch on one coat, let the canvas dry, and then do a second coat. Pay special attention to the seams and corners.

WATERPROOFING SOAK FOR TENTS

This option is messier than the spray, but if you'd rather dip your tent, here you go:

<u>Step 1</u>: Dissolve <u>a pound of</u> <u>laundry soap</u> (use a store-bought one with detergents in it) in <u>two gallons of hot water</u>. Stir well, until the soap bits are totally dissolved. Dunk your whole tent in the liquid, wring out the excess, and then dry it on a line or on the ground in a sunny spot.

<u>Step 2</u>: Dissolve <u>a half pound of alum</u> (check the hardware store) in <u>two more gallons of hot water</u>. Dunk the tent again and this time let it sit for a few hours. Wring it and let it air dry.

For maximum waterproofage, you should repeat this process every couple of months (if you use your tent often) or whenever you feel like it's getting leaky.

WATERPROOFIN' LEATHER

Lanolin is an oily substance derived from sheep's wool. It's an excellent waterproofer and pretty eco-friendly, too. (Just do a little research when you're shopping to make sure your lanolin is humanely obtained.) To use it, rub a bit into the leather with a soft cloth. Keep buffing until the leather feels dry (not greasy) to the touch. This also keeps the leather supple, which is nice.

If you have leather stuff but desire non-animal-derived waterproofing for it, petroleum jelly is a decent option. It's not earth-friendly, of course, but it's effective and cheap.

NOTE: Don't use either of these on suede — the oils will ruin the suede's nap. Honestly, suede is such a pain in the ass. Don't wear suede.

WATERPROOFING LIGHT NATURAL FABRICS
linen, hemp, and light canvas

NOTE: This may change the texture or appearance of your fabric.

Step 1: Gather a disposable paintbrush, some paper towels, a clean rag, and some beeswax.

Step 2: Melt the wax (stove or microwave) and paint it onto your fabric. Use paper towels to mop up leftover wax in the pan while it's still warm.

Step 3: Let the wax set overnight — I suggest laying it on a layer of old paper bags — and in the morning, buff the fabric with the rag.

WATERPROOFING NYLON

To waterproof nylon, you can use <u>beeswax</u> and the same method as for light natural fabrics. It might help to stuff the legs or arms with plastic while you're applying the wax, so that the hardening wax won't "glue" the layers of fabric together.

You also have your choice of vegan alternatives! <u>Linseed oil</u> or <u>jojoba oil</u> can be applied to a clean rag and then buffed in to the nylon. Let the fabric sit overnight (or until it feels dry) and apply more coats if you so desire.

NOTE: You can get linseed oil from the hardware store and jojoba oil from the body care section of the health food store. If you decide to use linseed oil, make sure it's 100% pure linseed oil without any chemicals added. Also, linseed oil makes fabric stiff and sort of unattractive, so it's probably better for a backpack, bike cover, or tarp.

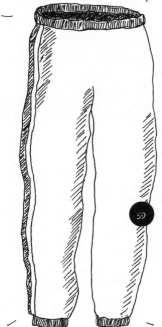

☆ waterproof ☆ jogging pants!

Sewing +

Mending

Resources

<u>Martha Stewart's Encyclopedia of Sewing</u>
<u>and Fabric Crafts</u> (really, it's great)
by Martha Stewart
New York: Potter Craft, 2010

<u>Stitch 'n' Fix: Essential Mending Know-</u>
<u>How for Bachelors and Babes</u>
by Joan Gordon
Lewes: Guild of Master Craftsman, 2009

<u>Very Basic Book of Sewing, Altering, and</u>
<u>Mending</u>: 999 Pictures Show You How
by Violet Kathleen Simons
New York: Sterling Pub. Co., 1976

www.learningalterations.com